URSA

Where You DARE Not Go

# Wretched Residences

SCARY MANORS AND MANSIONS

by
Joyce Markovics and
Dinah Williams

Minneapolis, Minnesota

## Credits

Cover and title page, © Perry/Adobe Stock and © Lightfield Studios/Adobe Stock and © Drasa/Adobe Stock and © iploydoy/Adobe Stock and © sergofan2015/Adobe Stock and © Juha Saastamoinen/Adobe Stock and © Elena Schweitzer/Adobe Stock and © Eric Isselée/Adobe Stock ; 4–5, © Tim Berghman/Adobe Stock and © Kathy/Adobe Stock and © Indiloo/Adobe Stock and © Brent/Adobe Stock; 6, © Public domain/Wikimedia; 7TR, © Public domain/Wikimedia; 7B, © Leigh Prather/Adobe Stock; 8, © Sean Pavone/Shutterstock; 9TR, © Public domain/Wikimedia; 9BR, © grape_vein/Adobe Stock; 10, © James Talalay/Alamy Stock Photo; 11TR, © James Talalay/Alamy Stock Photo; 12, © Gestalt Imagery/Shutterstock; 13MR, © Master1305/Shutterstock; 14, © DnDavis/Shutterstock; 15BL, © poco_bw/Adobe Stock; 15BR, © Enrico Della Pietra/Shutterstock; 16, © PA Images/Alamy Stock Photo; 17BR, © KUCO/Shutterstock; 18, © Giacomo Guidetti/Alamy Stock Photo; 19BR, © borisblik/Adobe Stock; 20, © Timothy Mulholland/Alamy Stock Photo; 21TR, © Public domain/Wikimedia; 22, © Public domain/Wikimedia; 23BR, © Library of Congress; 24, © DMBrooks/Shutterstock; 25TR, © ART Collection/Alamy Stock Photo; 26, © Craig Hinton/Shutterstock; 27TR, © Public domain/Wikimedia; 28, © Matthew Kiernan/Alamy Stock Photo; 30, © PhotoFires/Shutterstock; 31BR, © Andrey Kiselev/Adobe Stock; 32, © Wangkun Jia/Alamy Stock Photo; 33TR, © Public domain/Wikimedia; 34, © Acroterion/Wikimedia; 35TR, © Pictorial Press Ltd/Alamy Stock Photo; 35BR, © Public domain/Wikimedia; 36, © 4kclips/Shutterstock; 37TR, © Public domain/Wikimedia; 38, © Christopher Busta-Peck/Wikimedia; 39B, © Bearport Publishing; 40, © shalaby/Wikimedia; 41TR, © Mohamed El-Shahed/Getty Images; 42–43, © Triff/Shutterstock

## Bearport Publishing Company Product Development Team

Publisher: Jen Jenson; Director of Product Development: Spencer Brinker; Managing Editor: Allison Juda; Editor: Cole Nelson; Associate Editor: Naomi Reich; Associate Editor: Tiana Tran; Designer: Kim Jones; Designer: Kayla Eggert; Product Development Specialist: Owen Hamlin

## Statement on Usage of Generative Artificial Intelligence

Bearport Publishing remains committed to publishing high-quality nonfiction books. Therefore, we restrict the use of generative AI to ensure accuracy of all text and visual components pertaining to a book's subject. See BearportPublishing.com for details.

Library of Congress Cataloging-in-Publication Data is available at www.loc.gov or upon request from the publisher.

ISBN: 979-8-89577-096-2 (hardcover)
ISBN: 979-8-89577-213-3 (ebook)

Copyright © 2026 Bearport Publishing Company. All rights reserved. No part of this publication may be reproduced in whole or in part, stored in any retrieval system, or transmitted in any form or by any means, electronic, mechanical, photocopying, recording, or otherwise, without written permission from the publisher. Bearport Publishing is a division of FlutterBee Education Group.

For more information, write to Bearport Publishing, 5357 Penn Avenue South, Minneapolis, MN 55419.

# Contents

Horror in the House? . . . . . . . . . . . . . . . . . . . . . . . . . 4

Phantom Fires . . . . . . . . . . . . . . . . . . . . . . . . . . . . . . 6

Old House, Old Ghost . . . . . . . . . . . . . . . . . . . . . . . 8

Sinister Spirits . . . . . . . . . . . . . . . . . . . . . . . . . . . . 10

"Come Play with Me" . . . . . . . . . . . . . . . . . . . . . . . 12

Misery at Dusk . . . . . . . . . . . . . . . . . . . . . . . . . . . . 14

Chased from Their Mansion . . . . . . . . . . . . . . . . . . 16

The Ghost Mansion . . . . . . . . . . . . . . . . . . . . . . . . 18

Axe Murder at an Architect's Home . . . . . . . . . 20

Footsteps in the Night . . . . . . . . . . . . . . . . . . . . . 22

A Horrible Hostess . . . . . . . . . . . . . . . . . . . . . . . . 24

Double Murder . . . . . . . . . . . . . . . . . . . . . . . . . . . 26

Mob Murder in a Haunted Mansion . . . . . . . . 28

The Green Lady . . . . . . . . . . . . . . . . . . . . . . . . . . . 30

Salem's Sheriff . . . . . . . . . . . . . . . . . . . . . . . . . . . . 32

Ghostly Gallows . . . . . . . . . . . . . . . . . . . . . . . . . . . 34

California's Most Haunted . . . . . . . . . . . . . . . . . . 36

Death and More Death . . . . . . . . . . . . . . . . . . . . 38

A Dark Dream . . . . . . . . . . . . . . . . . . . . . . . . . . . . 40


A World Full of . . . Wretched Residences . . . . 42

Glossary . . . . . . . . . . . . . . . . . . . . . . . . . . . . . . . . . 44

Read More . . . . . . . . . . . . . . . . . . . . . . . . . . . . . . . 46

Learn More Online . . . . . . . . . . . . . . . . . . . . . . . . 46

Index . . . . . . . . . . . . . . . . . . . . . . . . . . . . . . . . . . . . 47

# Horror in the House?

Old houses hold an undeniable charm, reminding us of lively stories from the past. We wonder about all that may have happened in these homes. But with echoing footsteps and mysterious voices, wonder can quickly turn to fear. Perhaps the past hasn't quite finished and is demanding to still be seen and heard in the present. . . .

# Phantom Fires

## THE DRISH HOUSE
## TUSCALOOSA, ALABAMA

For decades, the Drish House was left to rot. It became a crumbling shell of the elegant home it once was. Some believe that the spirit of the mansion's former owner dwells there—and that she sets the house ablaze every night.

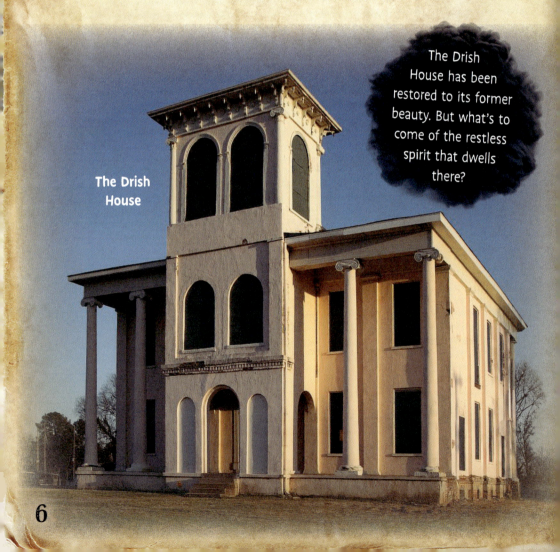

The Drish House

The Drish House has been restored to its former beauty. But what's to come of the restless spirit that dwells there?

John Drish and his wife, Sarah, began building their large house in 1837. It had a central tower, tall columns, and ornate plasterwork. The couple lived happily in the mansion until one evening in 1867. According to one story, John began stumbling and acting strangely before falling to his death from the upstairs balcony.

The Drish House in 1905

Sarah was overcome with grief, and to busy herself, she spent all of her time planning her husband's funeral. Every detail had to be perfect, even the candles. After John was buried, Sarah never recovered and often thought about her own death. She became fixated on having the exact same funeral as her husband. The candles used at his funeral, she stated, must be reused at her own funeral. When Sarah died in 1884, however, no one could find the candles for the funeral, and her request was not carried out.

Soon after, a passerby saw a fire burning in the mansion's tower. When firefighters arrived, there was no fire. The phantom fires still continue day after day. Some believe Sarah's restless spirit is responsible for the ghostly blazes. Is she still grieving for John and upset about the lost candles?

# Old House, Old Ghost

## THE MORRIS-JUMEL MANSION
## NEW YORK, NEW YORK

Many famous people visited the New York mansion that became known as Mount Morris. In 1776, George Washington used it as his headquarters while he was fighting the British during the Revolutionary War (1775-1783). In 1790, Washington dined there with future presidents John Adams and Thomas Jefferson. Of course, none of these famous visitors stayed nearly as long as homeowner Eliza Jumel.

Morris-Jumel Mansion

Wealthy French wine merchant Stephen Jumel bought Mount Morris—which would become known as the Morris-Jumel Mansion—with his wife, Eliza, in 1810. In 1832, Jumel fell from a carriage and was seriously injured. He died shortly after, leaving Eliza his vast fortune. Not everyone believed the accident had killed him, though. People whispered that Eliza had loosened the bandages that covered his wounds, causing him to bleed to death.

**Eliza Jumel**

The rumors didn't stop when Eliza married former vice president Aaron Burr a short time later. After Burr's death in 1836, Eliza lived alone in the mansion and started acting strangely. Some said she lost her mind before dying in 1865 at the age of 90. In 1904, the house became a museum, and since then people have claimed to see Eliza's ghost wandering the halls. Reportedly, she wears a purple dress and knocks loudly on doors and windows.

During a 1964 visit to the mansion, schoolchildren were playing and making noise on the lawn. A woman soon came out on the balcony and told them to be quiet. Based on the clothing she was wearing, the woman was later identified as the ghost of Eliza Jumel.

# Sinister Spirits

## MONTE CRISTO HOMESTEAD
## JUNEE, AUSTRALIA

Built in 1885, this elegant Victorian house sits on a hill overlooking the town of Junee. Could it be the most haunted house in Australia? Olive Ryan, one of the owners, knew the answer to that question the moment she set foot on the property.

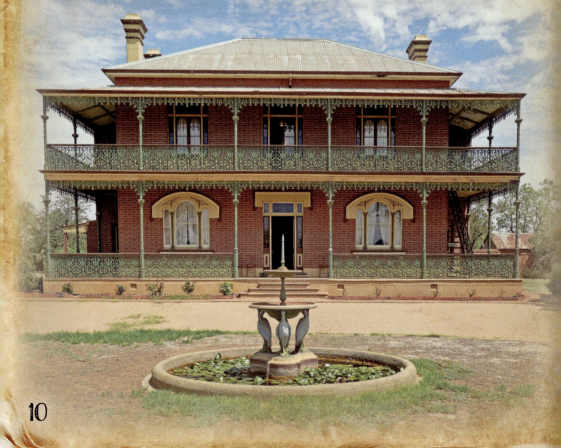

Monte Cristo Homestead

In 1963, Olive Ryan and her husband first arrived at their new house. Blinding light was shining from inside it, even though the electricity wasn't yet hooked up. This was the first of many spooky stirrings at Monte Cristo.

**A room inside the Monte Cristo Homestead**

When the Ryan family began to look into the home's history, they grew even more unsettled. They discovered that a baby had died in the house. Supposedly, it had been yanked from the arms of a nanny by an unseen force and thrown down the stairs. Other stories tell of a boy who burned to death in the barn and a maid who jumped off the balcony to her death.

Olive Ryan had countless terrifying experiences of her own, including hearing her name called and feeling an unseen hand on her shoulder. She also heard footsteps on the balcony from which the maid is said to have jumped. For years, the Ryan family welcomed visitors to come see for themselves if the mansion really is spilling over with spirits.

The Ryans say they have also seen the Monte Cristo's long-dead original owners, Christopher and Elizabeth Crawley, in the house. White, shadowy figures thought to be the Crawleys also appear in photos taken inside the home.

# "Come Play with Me"

## KEHOE HOUSE
### SAVANNAH, GEORGIA

Tourists in Savannah's historic district expect to see cobblestone streets, beautiful mansions, and moss-covered oak trees. What they don't expect is to hear otherworldly voices calling, "Play . . . come play with me." Could these voices coming from the Kehoe House be those of ghostly children looking for playmates?

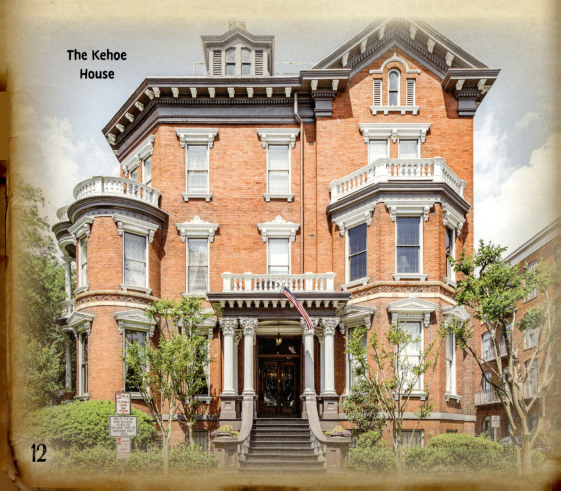

The Kehoe House

In 1892, wealthy businessman William Kehoe built a mansion large enough for his 10 children. The five-story redbrick building, which still stands today, has more than a dozen bedrooms. There are brass and marble chandeliers, a courtyard garden, and 18 fireplaces. According to legend, two of the Kehoe children met their end in one of these fireplaces. The twin boys are said to have died in an accident while playing in the chimney. After their deaths, the fireplace mantel was decorated with angels in their memory.

William Kehoe died in 1929, and the house was sold a year later. Since then, it has become a luxurious inn—with some ghostly guests! Visitors have heard children running and playing in the halls at night even when no children were staying at the inn at the time. One night, a guest in room 201 awoke when she felt a small hand on her cheek. She opened her eyes to the sight of a young boy, who quickly disappeared. Was he playing a ghost's version of hide-and-seek?

William Kehoe's favorite spot in the house was the cupola. A light has been seen burning there late at night. People say the light comes from a ghostly Kehoe—still working late into the night even after his death.

# Misery at Dusk

## BOONE HALL PLANTATION
## MT. PLEASANT, SOUTH CAROLINA

Boone Hall is one of the oldest working plantations in the United States. Dating from 1681, the property includes a brickyard and nine small cabins that once housed hundreds of enslaved workers. Sometimes, as the sun sets at Boone Hall, the horror that took place there long ago comes alive.

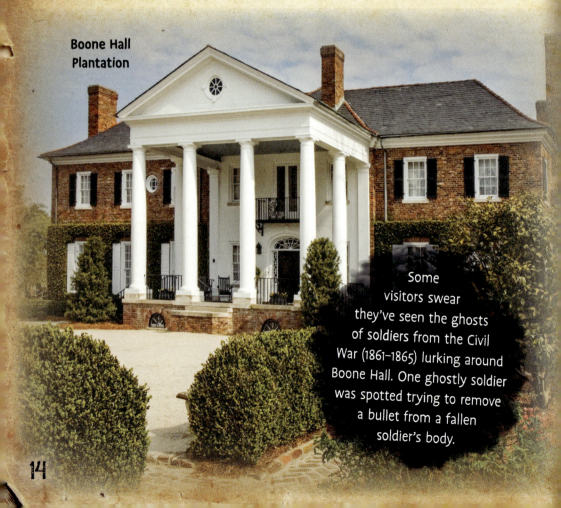

Boone Hall Plantation

Some visitors swear they've seen the ghosts of soldiers from the Civil War (1861–1865) lurking around Boone Hall. One ghostly soldier was spotted trying to remove a bullet from a fallen soldier's body.

Horribly, the Boone Hall plantation enslaved as many as 225 people at its busiest. In addition to being forced to grow cotton and other crops, many of the people also had to work at the property's brickyard. Making bricks was dangerous and backbreaking work. The workers had to dig up clay from a nearby creek and form it into bricks. To harden the bricks, the workers baked them in a giant, fiery oven called a kiln. Since this was often done at dusk when it was hard to see, accidents were all too frequent. Many were burned alive by the flames that poured out of the kiln.

Since that time, a ghost has been seen in the brickyard at dusk. She's hunched over and dressed in ragged clothes. She moves her hands in a repeated thrusting motion as though under a spell. Is the apparition an enslaved worker who lost her life in the brickyard's inferno?

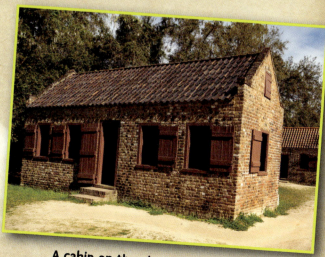

A cabin on the plantation that housed enslaved workers

# Chased from Their Mansion

## CLIFTON HALL
### NOTTINGHAM, ENGLAND

More than 700 years ago, Clifton Hall started out as a small stone house. However, its owners expanded the building over the centuries to include 52 rooms. Among them are 17 bedrooms, a gym, a movie theater, and 10 bathrooms. So why does this huge and historic mansion stand empty? According to one of its recent owners, there is a simple answer—ghosts.

Clifton Hall

Millionaire Anwar Rashid moved into Clifton Hall with his family in 2007. During their first night there, family members heard someone pounding on the walls. Then, an unknown man's voice said, "Is anyone there?" After a long search, the Rashids couldn't find anyone in the house. A few months later, Anwar's wife saw what looked like her daughter downstairs at 5:00 a.m. Yet, when she checked the girl's room, she was asleep in her bed.

For eight months, the family was pestered by spirits—or at least by unexplained sights and sounds. Finally, when Mr. and Mrs. Rashid found drops of blood on their baby's quilt, the strange happenings became too much for them. They fled the house and have never returned. After the horrible ordeal, Anwar Rashid said, "The ghosts didn't want us there, and we could not fight them because we couldn't see them."

During their stay, the family called paranormal investigators, but these experts could not drive the spirits from the house. In fact, two investigators fainted after seeing the ghost of a boy.

# The Ghost Mansion

## VILLA DE VECCHI
## LAKE COMO, ITALY

Nestled in the mountains of Italy is Villa de Vecchi, also known as The Ghost Mansion. Its empty windows look like soulless eyes. How did this once-grand house become a dwelling for ghosts?

Villa de Vecchi

In 2002, Villa de Vecchi was almost destroyed by an avalanche.

In the 1850s, a nobleman named Felix de Vecchi decided to build a summer home for his family near Lake Como. He hired Alessandro Sidoli to design and build a four-story mansion. The house included a stunning fountain, huge fireplaces, and a grand hall that held a piano. However, a year before it was finished, Sidoli passed away. Some people think his death may have set into motion a terrible curse.

It's said that years later, de Vecchi returned home one day to a scene of horror. He stumbled upon the dead body of his wife with her face badly disfigured. He also found that his beloved daughter had been kidnapped. For a long while, Felix searched for his child, but sadly, he never found her. Felix's sadness soon spiraled out of control. Unable to deal with the terrible losses, he took his own life in 1862. He was just 46 years old.

Today, people walking by the mansion often hear the eerie sound of a piano coming from inside the home's crumbling walls. Is it Felix's spirit tapping the keys in never-ending sorrow?

# Axe Murder at an Architect's Home

## TALIESIN
### SPRING GREEN, WISCONSIN

Famed architect Frank Lloyd Wright fell in love with a woman named Mamah Borthwick in 1909. He built her a beautiful home, where he hoped they would grow old together. Instead, it became the site of her murder.

Taliesin

Taliesin, which means shining brow in Welsh, is the name Frank Lloyd Wright gave to the mansion he built for Mamah Borthwick. The name is fitting, since the long building was perched on the brow of a hill overlooking the Wisconsin River. In 1911, Wright moved in with Borthwick and her two children.

Mamah Borthwick

On August 15, 1914, Wright had to travel to Chicago on business. When Borthwick, her children, and some workers went inside the house for lunch, the Wright family's butler, Julian Carlton, was waiting. He locked the dining room doors and set fire to the room. Carlton used an axe to attack anyone who tried to escape the flames. He killed seven people, including Mamah Borthwick and her children. Later, firefighters took their bodies to a cottage on the property.

Borthwick was buried on the grounds of Taliesin. Over the next few years, Wright rebuilt the mansion. Since that time, Borthwick's spirit has been seen by many visitors. She is said to wander near the cottage where her body was taken after the fire.

Taliesin was destroyed again by an electrical fire in 1925. It was rebuilt a final time and served as Wright's studio. Here, he designed his most famous buildings—the Guggenheim Museum in New York and Fallingwater in Pennsylvania.

21

# Footsteps in the Night

## ROCKLIFFE MANSION
### HANNIBAL, MISSOURI

Rockliffe Mansion is a 13,500-square-foot (1,254-sq-m) home that was built on high, rocky ground above the city of Hannibal. Visitors to the house are transported back in time . . . and, perhaps, to a world in which spirits exist.

Rockliffe Mansion

A businessman named John J. Cruikshank built Rockliffe Mansion in the late 1890s. In 1924, Cruikshank died in his bed. For the next 43 years, the house sat empty, falling into ruin.

In the 1960s, the city of Hannibal had plans to tear down Rockliffe. Just before the bulldozers arrived, townspeople went inside the old house and found beautiful antique lamps, rugs, art, and bedsheets. Eerily, the bedroom where Cruikshank had died was untouched. Inspired, a group of local residents decided to buy the mansion and restore it. At the time, they had no idea the house was a hangout for ghosts.

On several occasions, caretakers have seen the indentation of a body in Cruikshank's bed. People have repeatedly heard phantom footsteps. One night, one of the caretakers waited and listened as the ghostly footsteps grew louder. Then, when the footsteps finally reached her, she felt a rush of cool air blow past her face. Was it Cruikshank's spirit making its nightly rounds?

The famous writer Mark Twain was raised in Hannibal and was a friend of John J. Cruikshank's. Twain visited Rockliffe Mansion frequently.

Mark Twain in front of his childhood home

# A Horrible Hostess

## LALAURIE HOUSE
## NEW ORLEANS, LOUISIANA

No one passed up an invitation to Madame Lalaurie's house. She was a rich, important person in New Orleans during the early 1800s, and she threw fancy parties where people danced and dined. However, while the music played and guests enjoyed themselves, they had no idea of the horrors their hostess hid from them in the attic above.

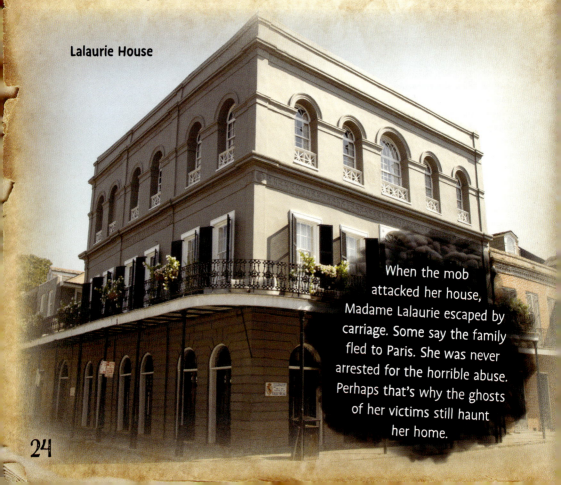

Lalaurie House

When the mob attacked her house, Madame Lalaurie escaped by carriage. Some say the family fled to Paris. She was never arrested for the horrible abuse. Perhaps that's why the ghosts of her victims still haunt her home.

Dr. Louis Lalaurie and his wife, Delphine, moved into their beautiful three-story mansion in 1832. Although dozens of enslaved workers would spend all day keeping it clean, Madame Lalaurie was never satisfied. To show her displeasure, she would beat the workers—and worse.

Madame Lalaurie

In 1834, when a fire broke out in the house, rescuers raced through the rooms. When they reached the attic, they crashed through a locked door. There, they found startling evidence of Madame Lalaurie's horrible cruelty: enslaved people were chained to the walls. They had been beaten and were weak with hunger. One man had open wounds all over his body.

Newspapers reported the terrible discovery, and the people of New Orleans were shocked. They wanted Madame Lalaurie to pay for her horrific crime. When they couldn't find her, a mob descended on the mansion, nearly destroying the inside of the house.

As the years passed, the building became a school, a bar, and finally, an apartment house. Despite the changes, however, the ghostly screams of Madame Lalaurie's victims were still heard within its walls. Today, the Lalaurie mansion is still said to be one of the most haunted places in New Orleans.

# Double Murder

## GLENSHEEN
### DULUTH, MINNESOTA

Many people insist that this 39-room estate isn't haunted. However, the piercing screams and glowing orbs might suggest otherwise. Could the fact that the house was the site of a double murder explain the eerie events?

Glensheen mansion

When Elisabeth Congdon's father died, she inherited his fortune and Glensheen mansion. After raising her two children, Marjorie and Jennifer, Congdon enjoyed spending her final years at the mansion under the care of her nurse. Then, tragedy struck. On June 27, 1977, a worker spotted two legs dangling from a staircase landing and saw the nurse's lifeless body in a pool of blood. A heavy brass candlestick lay nearby. When the worker continued to Congdon's room, what she saw took her breath away. Congdon, too, was dead. She had been smothered with a satin pillow. Who could have carried out such an evil act?

Elisabeth Congdon

After Congdon's death, her daughter Marjorie was to receive $8 million. Many people believe she wanted the money and was willing to kill to get it. However, there wasn't any proof that Marjorie was guilty of the murders. Today, some visitors to Glensheen have been shaken by loud screams and moans in the night. Others have seen ghostly orbs and clouds of mist appear in the library where Congdon enjoyed reading.

Marjorie's husband went to jail for the murders. He later took his own life. Did Marjorie get away with murder?

# Mob Murder in a Haunted Mansion

## KREISCHER MANSION
## STATEN ISLAND, NEW YORK

For many years, Charles Kreischer's mansion on Arthur Kill Road was thought to be haunted. Perhaps that's because of his family's tragic history. While their story is heartbreaking, it is not as terrible as what happened in the house a century later.

The Kreischer Mansion

Balthasar Kreischer moved his family from Germany to the United States in 1836. A year earlier, many of New York City's wooden buildings had been destroyed by a huge fire. As a result, Kreischer was able to make a fortune manufacturing fireproof brick from Staten Island clay. Around 1885, he built matching mansions on a hill for his sons, Charles and Edward.

During the 1890s, the series of terrible events began. First, the family's brick factory burned down. Then, with the business failing and much of the family fortune lost, Kreischer shot himself in the head. Finally, in 1930, Edward's house burned down, leaving the Charles Kreischer house the only mansion on the hill.

Many years later, in 2005, a man named Joseph Young was hired by the mansion's new owners to take care of the house while it was empty. Shockingly, Young's other job was working as an assassin for an organized crime group known as the Mob. A New York Mob boss hired Young to kill a man named Robert McKelvey. Young brought him to the mansion and carried out the murder there—drowning his victim in a pond that had been decorated with Kreischer bricks.

One ghost that has been said to haunt the Kreischer Mansion is Edward's wife, who can be heard crying over his death. Another is a cook who once worked for the Kreischers—and who is now heard clanging pots and pans.

# The Green Lady

### CHÂTEAU DE BRISSAC
### MAINE-ET-LOIRE, FRANCE

Château de Brissac looks like a castle from a fairy tale. However, if you look beyond its fancy facade, you will uncover a sinister story of betrayal and death.

Château de Brissac

In the 1400s, Jacques de Brézé lived in Château de Brissac with his wife, Charlotte. Their marriage, however, was not a happy one. One day, de Brézé flew into a rage when he found his wife with another man named Pierre de Lavergne. Then, on June 1, 1477, Charlotte and Pierre were found murdered. According to one story, Jacques de Brézé plunged his sword into their bodies more than 100 times. According to another, the angry husband strangled the lovers with his bare hands in a chapel in one of the castle's towers. No one knows for sure how they died, only that Charlotte and Pierre were never seen again.

Since the disappearances, a ghost believed to be Charlotte has been seen roaming the tower chapel. Early in the morning, her moans have been heard echoing through the castle. She appears to be wearing a flowing green gown, earning her the name The Green Lady. What startles people most of all is her corpselike face. There are huge gaping holes where her eyes and nose should be. ᴑᵧᴑ

Jacques de Brézé was arrested and jailed for the murders.

# Salem's Sheriff

## JOSHUA WARD HOUSE
## SALEM, MASSACHUSETTS

In 1692, more than 150 people in Salem were arrested on suspicion of witchcraft. Many of those accused were tortured until they confessed. Sheriff George Corwin got more than a confession from Giles Corey—he got a curse as well. Some say that curse may have left the sheriff unable to find rest. It may have even driven him to haunt a Salem mansion.

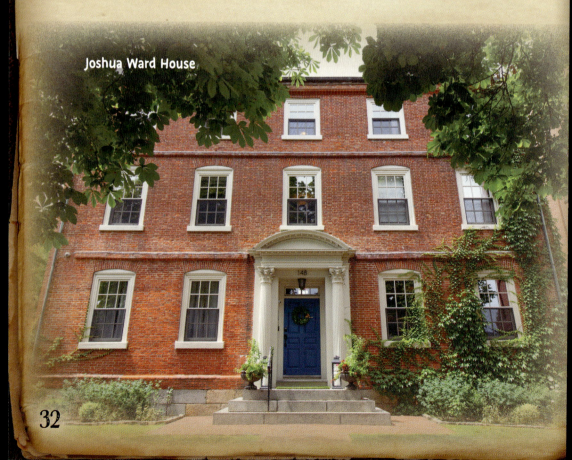

Joshua Ward House

George Corwin was the high sheriff of Essex County, and during the witch trials, he often forced confessions. One way he did that was to pile stones on the chest of the accused until he or she

*Giles Corey being crushed to death*

pleaded guilty. Giles Corey, an 80-year-old farmer, refused to tell a lie and say he practiced witchcraft. As a result, he was crushed to death by the weight of the stones. Some say he died cursing the cruel sheriff.

After causing so many deaths, Corwin died a hated man in 1696. So that no one could damage his body in revenge, he was originally buried in the basement of his home. In the 1780s, a wealthy sea captain named Joshua Ward built his mansion where Corwin's house had once stood. Corwin's ghost has reportedly been causing trouble inside the mansion ever since. Candles have mysteriously been melted and bent into the shape of an *S*. When the building was an inn during the late 1800s, guests reported seeing a man's ghost sitting by the fireplace. Later, when it was a business, the security alarm went off 60 times in 2 years without explanation.

In the 1980s, the mansion was used as a real estate office. When workers took a picture one day, they got a surprise. Instead of the employee, the picture showed a frizzy-haired woman in a long gray coat. Some believe it is the ghost of one of the accused witches sent to her death by George Corwin.

# Ghostly Gallows

## PERKINS HOUSE
## CHARLES TOWN, WEST VIRGINIA

Covered in a tangle of ivy sits a redbrick mansion dating from the 1800s. In the yard, there's an unusual carved stone beneath some trees. Most visitors would never guess that it marks the exact spot where the abolitionist John Brown dangled from a gallows.

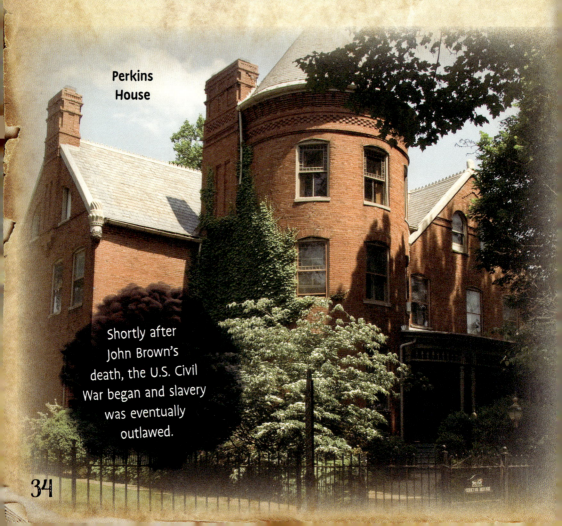

Perkins House

Shortly after John Brown's death, the U.S. Civil War began and slavery was eventually outlawed.

Born in Connecticut in 1800, John Brown believed that slavery was a horrible crime. For many years, he worked to peacefully put an end to it. However, despite his efforts, little changed in the United States. Brown believed more needed to be done—even if it meant taking violent action. On October 16, 1859, in Harpers Ferry, West Virginia, Brown planned an uprising of enslaved workers. He and a group of 21 men stole weapons from an arsenal. Brown was hoping that thousands of enslaved people would fight alongside him—but they never came. Although Brown and his men fought fiercely, they were no match for Colonel Robert E. Lee and his men. Brown was captured and thrown into prison.

John Brown

Weeks later, Brown was convicted of treason and sentenced to death. Before he died, Brown said he was glad to give up his life for the millions of enslaved people without rights. "So let it be done!" he shouted. On December 2, 1859, John Brown was hanged where the Perkins House now stands. Since that time, it's said that Brown's ghost has walked the property, still willing to fight for the cause he cared so deeply about.

John Brown at the gallows

# California's Most Haunted

## WHALEY HOUSE
### SAN DIEGO, CALIFORNIA

The Whaley House has stood on San Diego Avenue for more than 150 years. From the moment it was built where the city's old gallows once stood, it has reportedly been home to ghosts. In fact, so many visitors have seen spirits there that it's considered by some to be the most haunted house in California.

The Whaley House

In 1852, a man called Yankee Jim Robinson was sentenced to die for stealing a boat. Store owner Thomas Whaley was one of many present to see him hang. Four years later, Whaley built his two-story brick mansion on the empty lot where the gallows had once stood. Soon after his family moved in, heavy footsteps were heard in the house. Remembering what had happened at the site, Whaley became convinced that it was the ghost of Robinson.

**Thomas Whaley**

In 1960, Thomas Whaley's house became a museum. Since that time, not only Yankee Jim but also several other spirits from the Whaley family's days have appeared. Thomas's ghost has been spotted at the top of the stairs, while the ghost of his wife, Anna, has been seen both downstairs and in the garden. A long-haired girl is said to dart through the dining room. Legend has it that she was playing with the Whaley children in the backyard and broke her neck when she ran straight into the clothesline. Even the ghost of the Whaleys' dog has been seen running down the halls of the mansion.

Like Thomas Whaley, Yankee Jim is said to haunt the mansion's stairs. Eerily, the stairs are in the exact spot where the gallows once stood. Some visitors also claimed to have felt a noose tightening around their necks as they passed through the house.

# Death and More Death

## FRANKLIN CASTLE
## CLEVELAND, OHIO

Whirling lights, chilling cries, doors flying off their hinges—these are just some of the strange things visitors have reported at Franklin Castle. Could the ghostly events have anything to do with the mansion's mysterious past?

Franklin Castle

Hannes Tiedemann built Franklin Castle in 1881 for his wife, children, and mother. The stone mansion is topped with towers, giving it a castle-like appearance. It has more than 20 rooms, including a huge ballroom and—some believe—several secret passageways.

Not long after it was built, a string of mysterious deaths took place at the castle. In 1891, Tiedemann's mother and young daughter died within weeks of each other. During the next three years, Hannes and his wife buried three more children, the youngest child being just 11 days old. The cause of the children's deaths is unknown. When Tiedemann's wife passed away in 1895, neighbors began to wonder whether Hannes was involved in the deaths.

By 1908, the entire Tiedemann family, including Hannes, had died. When the bones of children were discovered in a cabinet in the house, people began to believe the rumors that Hannes was a murderer. Could there be another explanation for all the deaths?

According to a legend, Hannes might also have killed his young niece by hanging her from a beam in a secret room in the castle.

39

# A Dark Dream

## BARON EMPAIN PALACE
### CAIRO, EGYPT

Rising out of the Egyptian desert near Cairo is a sand-colored palace. The majestic house lures visitors in for a closer look. However, guests should beware. This old palace holds secrets that are better left in the dark.

Baron Empain Palace

Édouard Louis Joseph Empain, better known as Baron Empain, made millions of dollars building railroads in Europe. In 1904, he went on a trip to Egypt and fell in love with the country. He bought a large piece of land outside Cairo in order to build a grand home for his wife and daughter. In 1907, he began building a palace inspired by ancient temples in Cambodia. The main feature of the house was a huge tower that contained a spiral staircase. It's believed the staircase was built on a giant platform that spun all the way around.

The spiral staircase

Baron Empain's dream of a perfect house soon became a nightmare. One day, his wife tumbled down the spinning staircase and died. His distressed daughter then hid away in the dark basement. A few years later, she, too, was found dead in the palace.

Today, the empty palace is home to thousands of bats and—some say—ghosts. Shadowy spirits have been seen wandering through the house. Their ghostly voices can be heard as the bats take flight into the night sky.

In 1929, Baron Empain died. It's said that at the time of his death, mirrors in the palace dripped with blood.

# A World Full of...

- A double murder in Duluth, Minnesota
- A murdered mother in Spring Green, Wisconsin
- The bones of children in Cleveland, Ohio
- A cursed sheriff in Salem, Massachusetts
- Unexplained footsteps in Hannibal, Missouri
- A drowned victim in Staten Island, New York
- A house of spirits in San Diego, California
- A woman who lost her mind in New York, New York
- A phantom fire in Tuscaloosa, Alabama
- Haunted gallows in Charles Town, West Virginia
- Wails of suffering in New Orleans, Louisiana
- Spirits at sunset in Mt. Pleasant, South Carolina
- Ghostly children in Savannah, Georgia

# Wretched Residences

- Blood on a baby blanket in Nottingham, England
- The Green Lady in Maine-et-Loire, France
- A mournful musician in Lake Como, Italy
- The Staircase of Death in Cairo, Egypt
- A house of death in Junee, Australia

43

# Glossary

**ablaze** on fire

**abolitionist** someone who opposes slavery

**abuse** harmful treatment

**accused** blamed for or charged with a crime or doing something wrong

**apparition** a ghost or ghostlike image

**architect** a person who designs buildings and makes sure they are built properly

**arsenal** a place where guns and military equipment are stored

**assassin** a person who carries out a carefully planned murder

**avalanche** a large amount of snow, ice, or rock that suddenly moves down a mountain

**chapel** a small church

**Civil War** the U.S. war between the Southern states and the Northern states that lasted from 1861 to 1865

**confessed** admitted that one has done something wrong

**cupola** a round structure built on top of a roof

**curse** words spoken to cause evil or injury

**disfigured** changed or ruined by injury or some other cause

**distressed** troubled

**dwelling** a home or place to live

**eerie** mysterious, strange

**estate** a big house on lots of land

**facade** the front of a building

**funeral** a ceremony that's held after a person dies

**gallows** a wooden structure used to hang criminals

**gothic** gloomy or mysterious

**indentation** a deep cut or pit in something

**inferno** a large fire or a place that's like hell

**inherited** received something, such as money, from someone who has died

**inn** a small hotel

**legend** a story handed down from the past that may be based on fact but is not always completely true

**lures** attracts something

**lurking** secretly hiding

**luxurious** very comfortable and of high quality

**mansion** a very large and grand house

**mantel** a covering, which is often decorated, for a fireplace

**mob** a large group of angry people

**nobleman** someone who has a high social status

**noose** a large loop at the end of a piece of rope

**orbs** glowing spheres

**ordeal** a difficult experience

**organized crime** different kinds of illegal activities, such as robbery, gambling, and smuggling, planned and carried out by groups

**ornate** elaborately decorated

**paranormal investigators** people who study events or collect information about things that cannot be scientifically explained

**pestered** bothered or annoyed

**phantom** ghostly

**plantation** a large farm where crops such as cotton or tea are grown

**restore** to bring something back to its original condition

**rumors** stories that are told by many people but are not necessarily true

**sinister** dark or evil

**smothered** killed someone by covering their nose and mouth so they can't breathe

**spirits** supernatural creatures, such as ghosts

**stately** majestic

**suspicion** belief of guilt for a crime

**temples** religious buildings where people go to pray

**tragedy** a sad and terrible event

**treason** the act of overthrowing a government

**violent** acting with uncontrolled force

# Read More

**Blohm, Craig E.** *Ghost Tales and Hauntings.* San Deigo, CA: ReferencePoint Press, Inc., 2025.

**Giannini, Alex and Dinah Williams.** *Hauntings at Home: Scary Houses and Farms (Where You Dare Not Go).* Minneapolis: Bearport Publishing Company, 2025.

**Gitlin, Marty.** *The Eerie Tale of Lucy Hale's Haunted House (The Haunted Experiences of Celebrities).* Hallandale, FL: Mitchell Lane Publishers, 2025.

**Seigel, Rachel.** *The Haunted History of Chicago, Illinois (Haunted History of the United States).* Minneapolis: ABDO Publishing, 2024.

# Learn More Online

1. Go to **FactSurfer.com** or scan the QR code below.

2. Enter **"Wretched Residences"** into the search box.

3. Click on the cover of this book to see a list of websites.

# Index

Baron Empain 40-41
Baron Empain Palace 40
Boone Hall Plantation 14
Borthwick, Mamah 20-21
brickyard 14-15
Brown, John 34-35
Burr, Aaron 9
Carlton, Julian 21
castle 30-31, 39
Château de Brissac 30-31
Clifton Hall 16-17
Congdon, Elisabeth 27
Corey, Giles 32-33
Corwin, George 32-33
Crawley, Christopher and Elizabeth 11
Cruikshank, John J. 23
de Brézé, Jacques 31
de Vecchi, Felix 18-19
Drish House 6
Drish, John and Sarah 6-7
fires 6-7, 21, 25, 29, 42
Franklin Castle 38-39
funeral 7
gallows 34-37, 42
Glensheen 26-27
Green Lady, The 30-31, 43
Joshua Ward House 32
Jumel, Eliza 8-9
Jumel, Stephen 9
Kehoe House 12
Kreischer Mansion 28-29

Lalaurie, Delphine 24-25
Lalaurie House 24
Monte Cristo Homestead 10-11
Morris-Jumel Mansion 8-9
murder 20, 26-27, 29, 42
orbs 26-27
Perkins House 34-35
plantation 15
Rashid, Anwar 17
Revolutionary War 8
Robinson, Yankee Jim 37
Rockliffe Mansion 22-23
Ryan, Olive 10-11
Salem witch trials 32, 42
Sidoli, Alessandro 19
slavery 14-15, 25, 34-35
Taliesin 20-21
Tiedemann, Hannes 39
U.S. Civil War 14, 34
Villa de Vecchi 18
Whaley House 36
Whaley, Thomas 36-37
Wright, Frank Lloyd 20-21

47

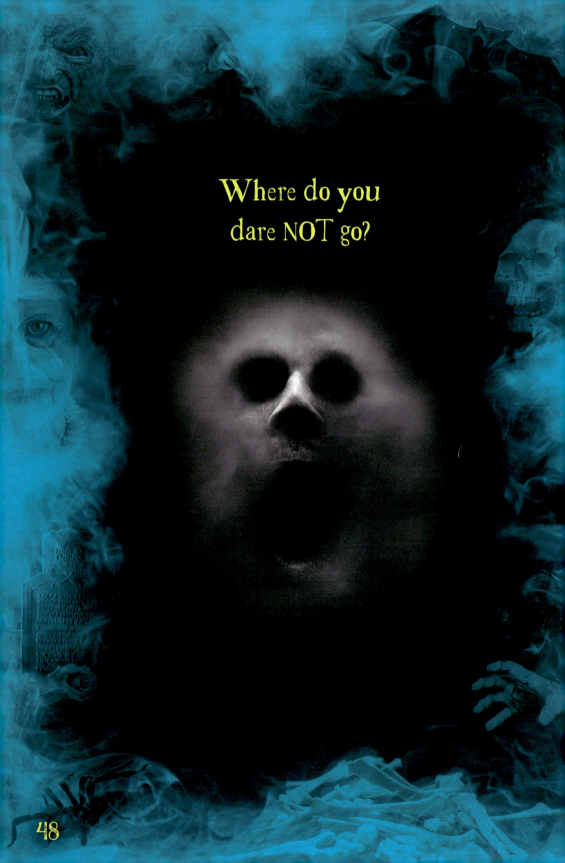